blue prints

Science Skills

Lawrie Ryan

Contents

How to use this book

This book contains a rich bank of resources to help children achieve their full potential in Science Attainment Target 1 (Sc1).

Teacher notes on pupil sheets

This section will develop your expertise in teaching the skills of scientific enquiry, as defined in the Revised National Curriculum Orders (September 2000). You will read the latest definition of scientific enquiry and look at the different ways of finding out the answers to scientific questions.

Using the new level descriptions, there is an analysis of the various skills that we need to promote as we teach science. Knowledge of this progression through the "skill strands" is the most important tool we have to help us differentiate activities in the classroom.

There are useful tips to prompt children's advancement via the "lines of progression"; there are also strategies that will challenge all children, at a level appropriate to the individuals in your class. The skill sheets, which form the body of the book, are analysed as to their National Curriculum level range and their links to the units in the QCA Scheme of Work. This helps you to use the sheets flexibly at any time during your course. For example, you may choose to introduce a particular skill sheet before an activity that requires that particular skill. You might use a sheet because of its contextual link to the unit of work being covered at the time; you may perhaps use a sheet to address an area of weakness identified during one of your science activities. The level range analysis will help you target sheets to the needs of individuals in your class, as they incorporate varying degrees of difficulty in each skill area.

Skill sheets

The main section of the book consists of skill sheets that enable children to practise the skills of scientific enquiry. These can be used in class to teach particular skills or as homework to develop skills met in class. They are not intended to be used as evidence for your teacher assessment of Sc1, which should take place in the context of normal enquiries in class. However, you are likely to gain useful diagnostic information that will inform your teaching. Addressing the children's needs in individual skills will raise their overall level of performance when they engage in actual scientific enquiry. The sheets will help to provide the "nuts and bolts" of scientific enquiry that children need in order to construct a whole investigation themselves at higher levels.

There are also historical case studies that show how scientific ideas have changed as a result of creative thinking or new experimental evidence. These will provide useful resources to meet some of the new requirements in the Sc1 Programme of Study.

Help sheets

In the final section you will find mechanisms that support writing in science. There are sheets that help you convert the theory of good assessment practice into reality in the classroom. This includes Sc1 "child-speak" criteria, designed to involve children in self-assessment and meaningful target setting in the classroom.

Teacher notes on pupil sheets

This section gives guidance and suggestions on how you might use the skill sheets and help sheets with your class.

The sheets are grouped according to the skill being developed. Where there is more than one sheet for a particular skill, the letter indicates the relative difficulty of the sheet (with Sheet (a) being the easiest). A detailed analysis of each sheet against the level of demand is given on pages xiv to xviii.

This table also includes a breakdown of each sheet in terms of the context in which the enquiry is set and its links to the relevant unit in the QCA Scheme of Work. This enables you to plan when to use particular sheets, possibly including references to them in your own Scheme of Work. However, the sheets can be used flexibly in that many of the skills being developed are essentially context-free. Practising the skills of measuring and recording do not rely on prior knowledge of content (but we should bear in mind that children will find it easier to access the sheets if they have recently used the skill in class). On the other hand, skills such as explaining predictions or conclusions are heavily dependent on scientific knowledge and understanding. These sheets should be used soon after the relevant content has been covered in class, although there is clearly scope for using such sheets when revising earlier work with Y6 children. You might consider using the sheets as support for starting off an enquiry (e.g. the sheets on asking questions, planning fair tests or predicting); they can also be useful in the demanding process of concluding and evaluating an investigation. These sheets can also assist children working at home, to allow more time in class for hands-on activities.

Let's look at the sheets written to help develop various Sc1 skills:

Skill sheets

Ideas and evidence

This topic area was introduced in the new National Curriculum in September 2000. The two sheets in this section are designed to stimulate discussion of the way scientists work and how breakthroughs are made. The work of Jane Goodall shows how success in the field often relies on the evidence of thousands of observations, painstakingly collected over many years. On the other hand, Edward Jenner shows the way that risk-taking and sudden insights, even hunches, play a role in advancing science.

Asking questions (and research)

Here we can build upon work in literacy and we can support children in constructing their own questions, using a variety of starting words. This strategy provides an excellent starting point for a topic, using the questions generated by the class as stimuli for enquiries later in the unit. It will be useful to consider how we could find the answers to some of the questions raised. This is meeting the demands of the broader definition of Sc1, which acknowledges that finding the answer to scientific questions does not solely rely on fair testing! Within the chosen contexts, many of the questions will need children to use secondary sources to find out the necessary information.

The children's experience of reading non-fiction texts in the literacy hour will be apparent as they embark on enquiries using their research skills, for example, using an index, making notes, etc. There is the opportunity for extended project work, which will be focused because it will be based on questions raised by the children themselves. Having considered the elements of non-fiction texts that the class appreciate, they can then work in groups to produce a project that will incorporate these features and present the results to the rest of the class. There are three help sheets in the book that can support this type of approach to research.

Predicting

The first sheet involves looking at magnets and it can be used with younger children; it encourages them to think ahead about what might happen in their tests. The blank row lets children choose another object to predict and test. This also helps to develop their recording skills. Extension work could be to ask children to draw their own table to record their predictions, and test another five objects.

The sheets that follow require children to use the knowledge and understanding they have gained to make their predictions, prior to tackling the investigations on friction or light. The final sheet adds a further level of demand, asking children to predict the shape of the line graph, with good links to numeracy skills.

Planning a fair test

Using a variety of contexts, the children are asked to list the relevant factors, choose one to investigate and plan a fair test. They need to be operating at Level 4 and above to tackle these planning activities independently, but working as a whole class or as groups / individuals with adult support gives access to children at lower levels.

These sheets can be used prior to tackling the practical activity. There are also a variety of help sheets to follow up these sheets or to support your class in any fair tests in your Scheme of Work.

Planning an enquiry

These sheets have been included to illustrate different aspects of scientific enquiry, other than the fair test. The first sheet on conductors and insulators is an example of a problem-solving activity. The second sheet is an investigation in a biological context in which it is difficult to control all the factors that might influence your testing. Finally, we have a sheet which aims to stimulate children to consider the different ways of finding the answers to our scientific questions.

Choosing equipment

These sheets can be used to encourage children to think ahead in their planning and select equipment (a Level 4 skill). You might do this in a planning session preceding your practical activity, collect in the suggestions made by groups and respond accordingly at the start of the next lesson where the focus will be on hands-on experimentation.

Measuring

Again the links with numeracy are apparent, with the emphasis in these sheets being on reading scales. The use of number lines and number sticks can be used to teach these skills. Sheets (b) and (f) actually give children the opportunity to measure length themselves. You could extend the scope of some of the sheets by asking for the results in Sheets (b), (d) and (f) to be put into a table, thereby developing recording skills.

Reliability

This sheet gives pupils a chance to practise Level 5 skills. The reliability of results can be improved in some investigations by taking repeat readings and calculating averages. Children should also recognise why this is necessary in some investigations but not others (not to be confused with "fair testing"); they need to be able to explain why there might be large differences in repeat readings. During an actual investigation, you will see children operating at higher levels, checking results again where they notice large differences in repeat readings.

Talking about ...

This sheet encourages younger children to share their ideas about how things move with each other. This is the first sheet in the Record / Present strand. The "Filling in charts" (Sheets (a)–(d)) will also be useful in these early stages of communicating results, which eventually leads to tables, bar charts and line graphs.

Sorting things into groups

Some enquiries will require children to classify objects or events into groups or sets. The first sheet provides the criteria for classification but the following sheets give children the opportunity to decide the criteria themselves – an approach you will be encouraging in Sc1 activities. The sheets also give practice in recording results in tables.

Filling in (and designing) charts and tables

The use of tables to record results systematically is a crucial recording skill in science. This series of sheets starts off by asking children to fill in simple charts. They progress to tables with just the headings provided, and are then required to choose their own headings. This skill is more difficult than one might think and children need lots of opportunities to develop it. These sheets could be useful for children who have missed the practical work associated with these investigations, through absence, or pupils who have been identified as having a weakness in this area. For extension work children can be asked to present the results shown in their tables (Sheets (b) and (c)) as bar charts.

The last two sheets on designing tables take the skill one step further by requiring the children to plan the layout, as well as deciding on the headings and filling in their tables. Children will find Sheet (e) particularly challenging as their table will have to accommodate repeat readings. Sheet (d) can be extended into bar chart work and Sheet (e) into a line graph.

Choosing how to record results

These two sheets give children a chance to decide which is the most appropriate way to show the results of different investigations. Using these sheets as teaching aids, you can start giving children the understanding of why we use bar charts in some investigations and line graphs in others. Use statements such as "We use bar charts when the factor we change in our investigation is described in words (not numbers)". This will help to give children more decision-making power in their own investigations.

Drawing bar charts

In order to access Level 4 in Sc1 pupils will need to be familiar with constructing and using bar charts. The skill should be developed as early as possible, using simple examples with adult support. Providing children with the labelled axes and getting them to draw on the bars will help. Pictograms and concrete representations will also assist them, such as charts made from lengths of string used to measure distance in an investigation. The sheets in this skill are differentiated according to the numeracy skills involved. They get more difficult as scaling becomes necessary and decimal numbers need to be recorded.

The sheets can be extended by asking children:

a How did you get these results?
b What conclusions can you draw from your bar chart?

Drawing line graphs

This skill is a development of the graphical recording skills practised in the previous section on bar charts. As with the bar charts, this work can be extended by asking for the plan or conclusion for the associated investigation. You could also give questions on reading from the finished graphs to make predictions (interpolation) or ask children to speculate on how the lines would carry on if the graphs were to be extended (extrapolation).

Concluding

The children start off by checking back against any predictions made. They interpret the results, bar charts, etc. They recognise and then describe any noticeable patterns (the ......er / more / less ......, then the ......er / more / less ......), using their scientific knowledge and understanding to explain patterns.

Evaluating

The final skill sheets cover the evaluation of enquiries, an area that makes an obvious contribution to the "thinking skills" initiatives in schools. The first two sheets challenge the concept of fair testing whilst the last sheet evaluates the strength of conclusions we can draw from an enquiry in a biological context – sample size being a critical factor in improving the validity of conclusions.

Help sheets

There are a variety of help sheets to support children in their enquiries. You can match these to the attainments of each child and use them as tools to aid differentiation. Remember that the ultimate writing frame is a blank piece of paper; similarly this is the case with the help sheets provided here. If children can do it themselves, then let them. If they can't, then using the help sheets will provide support and help children access activities that would otherwise lead to frustration and decrease motivation. The help sheets are useful teaching aids, with the aim being to wean the pupils off the sheets and give them the skills needed to become independent investigators.

Help sheets are provided to support:

- Researching (asking questions to focus the search for information, planning research and carrying out the research);
- Planning an investigation (a generic prompt sheet of ten questions children need to consider in their planning);
- Planning fair tests (a set of three sheets that will help children manipulate variables and understand how to record their results);
- Sorting things into groups (two sheets to record the results of classification activities);
- Recording results (a two-column table plus a more complex table for recording repeat readings);
- Concluding and evaluating (a generic prompt sheet of questions to consider at the end of any investigation).

The "child-speak" criteria for Sc1 are provided at a range of target levels. The theory is to involve children more in self-assessment, providing you with a method of sharing your learning objectives with them. This is never easy in an open-ended investigation where there will be significant differentiation by outcome. If we can get children involved in the self-assessment of Sc1 skills, then they will be able to set targets for themselves in the various skill strands and take a more active role in improving their skills. The child-speak criteria show them exactly what they need to do to progress to the next level in each particular skill.

You can read more about the skill strands that are essential to good science teaching and learning in the next few pages. A grid is included on page xiii for you to record children's attainment in Sc1 in each skill strand.

Progression in Sc1 Skills: lines of progression

The table below shows the level descriptions for Sc1, divided into five skill strands or "lines of progression".

	Research / Ideas and evidence	Plan / Predict	Observe / Measure	Record / Present data	Conclude / Evaluate
Level 1			Describe or respond appropriately to simple features of objects, living things and events they observe.	Communicate their findings in simple ways (e.g. talking about their work, through drawings, simple charts).	
Level 2	Use simple texts, with help, to find information.	Respond to suggestions about how to find things out and, with help, make their own suggestions about how to collect data to answer questions.	Use simple equipment provided and make observations related to their task; observe and compare objects, living things and events.	Describe their observations using scientific vocabulary and record them, using simple tables when appropriate.	Say whether what happened was what they expected.

Cont'd

viii

	Research / Ideas and evidence	Plan / Predict	Observe / Measure	Record / Present data	Conclude / Evaluate
Level 3	Recognise why it is important to collect data to answer questions. They use simple texts to find information.	Respond to suggestions and put forward their own ideas about how to find the answer to a question.	Make relevant observations and measure quantities, such as length or mass, using a range of simple equipment; where appropriate, can carry out a fair test with some help, recognising and explaining why it is fair.	Record their observations in a variety of ways.	Provide explanations for observations and for simple patterns in recorded measurements; they communicate in a scientific way what they have found out and suggest improvements in their work.
Level 4	Pupils recognise that scientific ideas are based on evidence; they select information from sources provided for them.	In their own investigative work, they decide on an appropriate approach (e.g. using a fair test) to answer a question; where appropriate, they describe, or show in the way they perform their task, how to vary one factor while keeping others the same; where appropriate, they make predictions; they select suitable equipment.	Make a series of observations and measurements that are adequate for the task; show in the way they perform their task, how to vary one factor while keeping others the same.	Record their observations, comparisons and measurements using tables and bar charts; begin to plot points to form simple graphs.	Use these graphs to point out and interpret patterns in their data; begin to relate their conclusions to these patterns and to scientific knowledge and understanding, and to communicate them with appropriate scientific language; suggest improvements in their work, giving reasons.

Cont'd

	Research / Ideas and evidence	Plan / Predict	Observe / Measure	Record / Present data	Conclude / Evaluate
Level 5	Describe how experimental evidence and creative thinking have been combined to provide a scientific explanation (e.g. Jenner's work on vaccination at Key Stage 2); select from a range of sources of information.	When trying to answer a scientific question, can identify an appropriate approach; when the investigation involves a fair test, can identify key factors to be considered; where appropriate, make predictions based on their scientific knowledge and understanding; select apparatus for a range of tasks and plan to use it effectively.	make a series of observations, comparisons or measurements with precision appropriate to the task; begin to repeat observations and measurements and to offer simple explanations for any differences encountered.	Record observations and measurements systematically and, where appropriate, present data as line graphs.	Draw conclusions that are consistent with the evidence and begin to relate these to scientific knowledge and understanding; make practical suggestions about how their working methods could be improved; use appropriate scientific language and conventions to communicate quantitative and qualitative data.

Gaining an insight into the criteria listed above is an essential part of a teacher's subject knowledge.

These "lines of progression" can be used for several purposes, which are outlined on the next pages.

Using the lines of progression

The table on the previous pages can be used to:

- introduce your school's portfolio of Sc1 evidence;
- improve reliability and consistency of teacher-assessed Sc1 levels;
- set meaningful learning targets for children in your class, and
- provide an insight into differentiation in science and how this can be applied in the classroom.

Portfolio of Sc1 evidence

A copy of the lines of progression should be kept in the front of your science portfolio so that visitors to the school or new members of staff know how your school makes its judgements.

Teachers often find it difficult to provide children's work illustrating a particular level in Sc1. This is not surprising when one looks at the range of skills required at each of the five levels. As written in the National Curriculum Orders, the level descriptions are very blunt instruments of assessment! However, the table on pages viii to x enables you to match pieces of work to distinct skill strands at any one particular level. It is much easier to recognise a Level 2 piece of recording, or a Level 5 prediction, etc. A brief annotation completes your evidence.

Teacher assessment of Sc1

Teachers are required to make a teacher assessment of science levels at the end of a key stage. The weighting given to Sc1 (50 per cent at Key Stage 1 and 40 per cent at Key Stage 2) makes it a vital component of accurate assessment.

The assessment criteria, as set out in the lines of progression, help to make the task of assessment much easier.

Setting meaningful targets

It is unlikely that a child will make perfectly even progress in each skill strand of Sc1. The lines of progression can provide a profile of performance. For example, a child in Y2 may have a strength in the Observe / Measure strand and be performing at Level 3, but have a relative weakness (Level 2) in the Conclude / Evaluate strand. Short-term targets can be drawn from the Level 3 criteria in the Conclude / Evaluate strand, for example "try to use your results to explain patterns". Other examples are: "try to use words from our Key Words for this topic when saying what you found out" and "try to think how you could make your investigations better".

For older children at Key Stage 2, the "child-speak" criteria at the end of this book can be used to give children access to self-assessment. This can also increase their involvement in setting their own targets for improvement.

Differentiation in science

The main advantage of an understanding of progression in Sc1 skills is improved differentiation in teaching science. When we look down each skill strand, we should be able to extract some general principles of progression. These will guide our teaching and enable us to pitch work at appropriately challenging levels for different groups of children. Therefore, expertise in Sc1 holds the key to effective differentiation in most of the activities we plan in science.

When engaged in teaching, you are not likely to find time to refer to the lines of progression, which is why we need to be familiar with the general principles of progression as a vital part of our subject knowledge. They can then be applied, not only in our planning, but also, and importantly, as opportunities arise in class.

The five skill strands: Progression

Research / Ideas and evidence
The level of support we give children decreases as we progress through the levels. They become more independent and draw from a wider range of resources to find out information.

Plan / Predict
As in the first strand, guidance given in planning is reduced as the level of demand increases.

Predictions should be developed from Reception onwards and every opportunity should be taken to ask children,"What do you think will happen?" and "Why?".

As we progress through the levels we will expect the reasoning to back up predictions. These will progress from those drawn from everyday experiences to those more firmly based in scientific knowledge and understanding. Although the word "prediction" is first mentioned at Level 4, children will find it more difficult to achieve Level 2 in Concluding (which requires them to check if what happened was what they expected) without a prediction!

Therefore, the degree of "open-endedness" is a key factor in determining the level pupils can achieve. By starting off with open-ended questions we allow access to higher levels in Sc1. Closed questioning will limit opportunities for pupils to use higher level skills. The guiding principle in these first two strands should be, "Start off open-ended, and close down tasks as necessary." We can then use teacher support as a tool to differentiate.

Observe / Measure

At the lower levels, there is a very useful line of progression going from Level 1 to Level 3, i.e.

Observe $\longrightarrow$ Compare $\longrightarrow$ Measure.

Those who can measure should be encouraged to do so. Children at Level 2 can sort and group things, and can put things in order. For example, they can sequence a number of cars after investigating "Which car rolls best?". But the numeracy skills needed to measure distances rolled, which are characteristic of Level 3, represent a large step for children. However, children can count before they can measure; encouraging children to use non-standard measures, such as counting the tiles on the floor that each car has travelled over, helps them work towards Level 3.

At higher levels the measurements become more precise and also more reliable. The concept of reliability ("If we were to do your tests again would we get the same readings?") is a Level 5 skill, but should be introduced much earlier in an appropriate way. For example, tests with younger children can be repeated to show that differences do occur, progressing to repeating a test three times and circling the middle number, leading to the averaging of readings typical of Level 5.

Record / Present

Starting from communicating observations by talking about them, this skill moves through simple tables (two columns), to bar charts and line graphs. As with measuring, the numeracy skills required for graph drawing need to be built up with support. For example, at Level 3 the descriptions are vague, i.e. results can be represented in a variety of ways. From the lines of progression we can see that Level 3 performance lies somewhere between the Level 2 simple table and the Level 4 bar chart. Applying the "level of support" evident in the first two strands, a bar chart with help could illustrate Level 3.

The question investigated becomes crucial to our strategy of differentiation in this strand. If the investigation is a "Which" test (such as, "Which paper towel is ...?" "Which trainer is ...?" "Which type of sugar ...?"), then the outcome will be a bar chart (Level 4). In order to challenge your higher attainers, the variable they change in an investigation should be continuous (i.e. measured), not categoric (i.e. described in words). This will then stimulate the skills of drawing line graphs (e.g. "Does the temperature affect how quickly sugar dissolves?").

Conclude / Evaluate

This strand relies on checking against any predictions made, looking for patterns in results, and explaining results, moving from everyday to scientific reasoning. The "thinking skills" needed to reflect on an enquiry and suggest improvements are also developed, with increased emphasis on justifying suggestions. Allowing time for these skills is important.

Progression in Sc1 skills: Class record for ....

Record the names or initials of children in the grid below (enlarge to A3 size when copying).

	Research / Ideas and evidence	Plan / Predict	Observe / Measure	Record / Present data	Conclude / Evaluate
Level 1					
Level 2					
Level 3					
Level 4					
Level 5					

Analysis of skill sheets by context, links to QCA Scheme of Work and level of demand

Sc1 Skills sheet	Context	Attainment target context	QCA unit	Level of Sc1 skill the sheet is aimed at:				
				Level 1	Level 2	Level 3	Level 4	Level 5
Ideas & evidence (a)	Habitats	Sc2	5 / 6H				○	●
Ideas & evidence (b)	Micro-organisms	Sc2	6B				○	●
Asking questions & research (a)	Worms	Sc2	4B		○	○	●	●
Asking questions & research (b)	Earth, Sun, Moon	Sc4	5F		○	○	●	●
Predicting (a)	Magnets	Sc3, Sc4	1C		●			
Predicting (b)	Friction	Sc4	4E		○	○	●	●
Predicting (c)	Shadows	Sc4	6F				○	●
Planning a fair test (a)	Forces	Sc4	2E		○	○	●	
Planning a fair test (b)	Materials	Sc3	3C		○	○	●	
Planning a fair test (c)	Parachutes	Sc4	4E		○	○	●	
Planning a fair test (d)	Evaporation	Sc3	5D		○	○	●	
Planning a fair test (e)	Shadows	Sc4	6F		○	○	●	

Cont'd

Sc1 Skills sheet	Context	Attainment target context	QCA unit	Level 1	Level 2	Level 3	Level 4	Level 5
Planning a fair test (f)	Electricity	Sc4	6G		○	○	●	
Planning an enquiry (a)	Electricity	Sc4	4F			●	○	○
Planning an enquiry (b)	Pulse rate	Sc2	5A			○	●	●
Planning an enquiry (c)	Moon	Sc4	5F			○	●	●
Choosing equipment (a)	Heat insulation	Sc3	4C			○	●	
Choosing equipment (b)	Dissolving	Sc3	6C			○	●	
Measuring (a)	Plants	Sc2	2C		●			
Measuring (b)	Materials	Sc3	2D / 3C			●	●	
Measuring (c)	Plants	Sc2	3B			●	●	
Measuring (d)	Weather / plants	Sc2	3B			●	●	
Measuring (e)	Forces	Sc4	4E / 6E			●	●	●
Measuring (f)	Parachutes	Sc4	4E			●	●	●
Measuring (g)	Elastic bands	Sc4	6E			●	●	●
Reliability (a)	Forces	Sc4	3E / 6E					●

Level of Sc1 skill the sheet is aimed at:

Sc1 Skills sheet	Context	Attainment target context	QCA unit	Level of Sc1 skill the sheet is aimed at:				
				Level 1	Level 2	Level 3	Level 4	Level 5
Talking about ... (a)	Forces	Sc4	1E	●				
Sorting things into groups (a)	Magnets	Sc3, Sc4	1C		●			
Sorting things into groups (b)	Floating / sinking	Sc3, Sc4	1C		●			
Sorting things into groups (c)	Minibeasts	Sc2	4B		●	●	●	
Filling in charts (a)	Human body	Sc2	1A	●				
Filling in charts (b)	Plants	Sc2	1B	●				
Filling in charts (c)	Light	Sc4	1D	●				
Filling in charts (d)	Sound	Sc4	1F	●				
Filling in tables (a)	Birds	Sc2	2B	○	●			
Filling in tables (b)	Magnets	Sc3, Sc4	1C	○	●			
Filling in tables (c)	Magnets	Sc3, Sc4	3E		●			
Filling in tables (d)	Forces	Sc4	4E			●	●	
Designing tables (a)	Absorbing water	Sc3	3C		○	●	●	●

Cont'd

Sc1 Skills sheet	Context	Attainment target context	QCA unit	Level of Sc1 skill the sheet is aimed at:				
				Level 1	Level 2	Level 3	Level 4	Level 5
Designing tables (b)	Spinners	Sc4	6E					●
Choosing how to record results (a)	Dissolving	Sc3	6C				●	●
Choosing how to record results (b)	Spinners	Sc4	6E				●	●
Drawing bar charts (a)	Forces	Sc4	2E			●		
Drawing bar charts (b)	Forces	Sc4	2E			○	●	
Drawing bar charts (c)	Friction	Sc4	4E			○	●	
Drawing bar charts (d)	Pulse rate	Sc2	5A			○	●	
Drawing bar charts (e)	Sound insulation	Sc4	5F			○	●	
Drawing line graphs (a)	Pulse rate	Sc2	5A				●	●
Drawing line graphs (b)	Dissolving	Sc3	6C				●	●
Drawing line graphs (c)	Springs	Sc4	6E				●	●
Drawing line graphs (d)	Shadows	Sc4	6F				●	●
Concluding (a)	Human body	Sc2	2A		●	●		
Concluding (b)	Forces	Sc4	2E		●	●		

Cont'd

Sc1 Skills sheet	Context	Attainment target context	QCA unit	Level 1	Level 2	Level 3	Level 4	Level 5
					Level of Sc1 skill the sheet is aimed at:			
Concluding (g)	Evaporation	Sc3	5D			●	●	●
Concluding (h)	Dissolving	Sc3	6C			●	●	●
Concluding (i)	Electricity	Sc4	4F / 6G			●	●	
Concluding (j)	Elastic bands	Sc4	6E			●	●	
Evaluating a fair test (a)	Forces	Sc4	2E			●		
Evaluating an enquiry (b)	Absorbing water	Sc3	3C			●		
Evaluating an enquiry (c)	Human body	Sc2	4A			●	●	●
Concluding (c)	Forces	Sc4	2E			●	○	○
Concluding (d)	Soils	Sc3	3D			●	●	●
Concluding (e)	Human body	Sc2	4A			●	●	●
Concluding (f)	Heat insulation (ICT)	Sc3, Sc4	4C			●	●	●

Ideas and evidence (a)
The work of Jane Goodall

Information sheet

Jane Goodall is a woman who has spent her life studying chimpanzees. She was inspired in her childhood by stories of Tarzan and Dr. Dolittle. It wasn't until 1957, when she was 23 years old, that she had saved enough money to travel to Kenya in Africa.

After a few years in Africa working on different tasks, she became a researcher, often working by herself, in a National Park in Tanzania. She planned to gather data on the chimpanzees that lived in the rugged, mountainous habitat. Some people doubted whether a young woman, who hadn't even studied at college, would find out anything very useful. At first, Jane herself wondered whether she could ever make any sense of her thousands of observations.

It took years of tracking and observing a group of chimps before she could really start to understand their "language" and behaviour. The world took notice when Jane's findings went against two commonly held beliefs. In the early 1960s most people thought that humans were the only animals who could make and use tools. However, Jane reported that chimps sometimes used grass to make "fishing lines" to gather berries that were difficult to reach. People also thought that chimps were vegetarians, but Jane observed chimpanzee hunting parties that would hunt smaller monkeys to kill and eat.

Her achievements were recognised in 1965 by Cambridge University. They awarded Jane an honorary doctorate. She continued to live in Tanzania until 1975, collecting more data on chimps that is still used by scientists today.

Nowadays, Jane is kept busy giving talks about her work with chimps and raising money for the chimpanzee refuges she has set up in Africa. She argues against using chimps, our closest relatives in the animal kingdom, for any medical research that is not absolutely essential. As she says, "It isn't only humans who have personality, who are capable of rational thought and emotions like joy and sorrow."
Britain has banned using apes for research.

Ideas and evidence (a)
Questions about Jane Goodall

Read the passage about Jane Goodall, then answer these questions:

1 Work out when Jane was born (to the nearest year).

....

2 What does the word "habitat" mean?

....

3 From which word do we get the word "chimp" ?

....

4 Why do you think it was difficult for Jane to gather data on the chimps?

....

....

5 Why did scientists start to take an interest in Jane's work?

....

....

6 Why do you think that medical companies might want to use chimps in their research? What are your views on this subject?

....

....

Name.. Date ....

Ideas and evidence (b)
The work of Edward Jenner (1749–1823)

Information sheet

Have you ever been vaccinated?
If you weren't too young, you probably
remember the needle!
You can thank Edward Jenner for
protecting you against many diseases.
He was the first person to show how to
inoculate safely against disease.

Smallpox was a disease that could kill
people and leave those lucky enough to
recover with lots of scars. It could be
passed on easily between people and
there was an epidemic in 1796.

Edward was a doctor in a village in
Gloucestershire, England. He noticed that farm workers who looked after
cows never caught smallpox. They were exposed to a much less serious
disease called cowpox. Edward had the idea that cowpox could somehow
protect people from getting the deadly smallpox.
But how could he show other people that he was right?

At this point he decided to try out a very dangerous experiment.
He persuaded a local farmer to let his son be infected with cowpox,
promising that this would protect the boy against smallpox.
Edward collected some puss from one of the sores on a milkmaid with
cowpox. He got the puss into young James Phipps by scratching his arm
and pouring the liquid on to the cuts. Sure enough, James had a mild
attack of cowpox.

Now came the big gamble! Six weeks later Edward did the same thing to
young James, but this time with puss from a smallpox sore. Fortunately,
Edward's theory was correct and the boy did not catch smallpox.

At first it was difficult to convince other people that introducing a mild
disease into your body could protect you against a more serious disease.
But it really did work, so doctors started to vaccinate people against
smallpox. The search was then on to find other diseases we could fight
using vaccination.

Nowadays, smallpox has been wiped out in this country, along with other
diseases, such as polio. Polio leaves children crippled. But vaccination
of all children in the 1950s and 1960s means that we are now safe from
the disease.

Ideas and evidence (b)
Questions about Edward Jenner

Read the passage about Edward Jenner, then answer these questions:

1 Where did Edward Jenner work as a doctor?

....

2 Which disease could Edward protect people against?

....

3 What do we call it when we introduce a little infection into the body to protect it against disease?

....

4 Why was Edward's experiment to test out his idea so risky?

....

....

5 Why do you think people found it hard to accept Edward's idea?

....

....

6 Imagine that you are Mr. Phipps, the farmer. Would you have given Edward permission to protect your son against smallpox?
Explain your answer.

....

....

Asking questions and research (a)

Worms are very interesting animals.

What would you like to find out about worms?

Make up some of your own questions.
Start each one with the words below:

Where ....

....

Why ....

....

How ....

....

What ....

....

If you can think of any other questions, write them on the back of this
sheet.

Now try to find the answers to some of your questions!

Name .... Date ....

6 Skill Sheet

Asking questions and research (b)

You are studying the Earth, Sun and Moon.

The Earth

The Moon

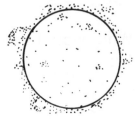

The Sun

(These drawings are not drawn to scale!)

Choose to find out more about the Earth, the Sun or the Moon.
Make up your own questions, starting with the words below:

Where ....

....

Why ....

....

How ....

....

What ....

....

When ....

....

Which ....

....

If you have time, write some more questions on the back of this sheet.

Now try to find the answers to some of your questions!

Predicting (a)

Which things do you think are magnetic?

Try another thing and fill in the bottom row of your table.

Things to test	Prediction: Do you think it is magnetic? (yes or no)	Now try out the test with a magnet. Were you right? (yes or no)
paper clip		
dice		
can		
ruler		

Predicting (b)

Two groups of pupils are finding out about friction.

Can you help them with their predictions?

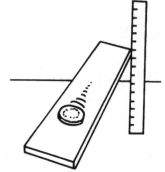

Group 1
They are investigating the question
"On which surface do objects slide most easily?"

They plan to test a slope covered with different surfaces.
They can use sandpaper, plastic, wood and carpet.

Which surface will be the most slippery? ....

Why? ....

....

Group 2
They are investigating the question
"Which shape travels fastest through water?"

They plan to use the same piece of plasticine.
They can mould this into different shapes.
Then they can time how long it takes each shape
to drop through a tube of water.
They plan to make the shapes below:

Water
in a tube ➔

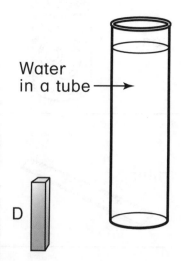

A 　　B ⬛　　C ⬨　　D ▯

Which shape will travel through the water most quickly? ....

Why? ....

....

Name.. Date ....

Predicting (c)

Kate's class are investigating light and shadows.

She is looking at what affects the size of a shadow.

She has set up the test shown below:

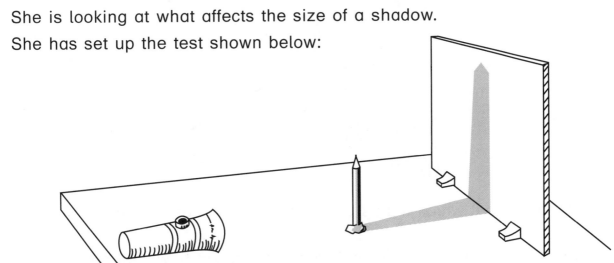

Kate wants to find out how changing the distance between the torch and the pencil affects the size of the shadow.

Can you help her make a prediction?

I think that ....

....

Sketch a line to show the pattern you think Kate will find.

Height of
shadow
(cm)

Distance between torch and pencil (cm)

Now try to explain your prediction by drawing a diagram on the back of this sheet.

Name .... Date ....

Planning a fair test (a)

Finding out about cars on slopes

You want to find out which things affect the way toy cars roll down slopes.

Make a list of all the things (factors) that might affect how well a car rolls.

....

....

....

....

....

....

Now choose one thing (factor) from your list to test.
Plan a **fair test** you could carry out in class.

....

....

....

....

....

Planning a fair test (b)

Finding out about tights

Sue says that she hates putting on her school tights in the winter.

"They are really hard to get your feet into," she moans.
"If only they were a bit more stretchy!"

"I know," says her friend Sami, "We'll test some different pairs of
tights to see which stretch most easily."

Can you help Sue and Sami investigate the problem:
"Which pair of tights is most stretchy?"

You have the equipment shown below:

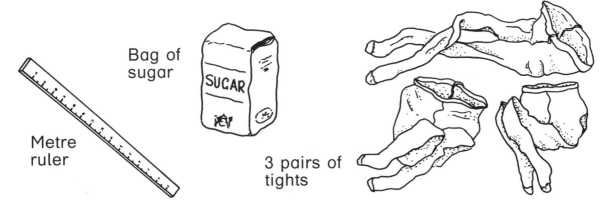

Bag of
sugar

Metre
ruler

3 pairs of
tights

Plan a **fair test** that Sue and Sami could try.

....

....

....

....

....

....

Planning a fair test (c)

Finding out about parachutes

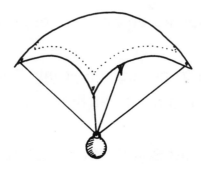

You want to find out what affects the way a parachute falls.

Make a list of all the factors that might affect how a parachute falls.

....

....

....

....

....

....

Now choose one factor from your list to test.
Plan a **fair test** to carry out in class.

....

....

....

....

....

Planning a fair test (d)

Finding out about evaporation

You have the equipment shown below:

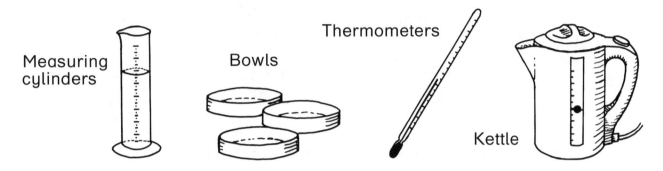

Measuring cylinders   Bowls   Thermometers   Kettle

You want to find out what affects how quickly water evaporates.

Make a list of the things (factors) that might matter.

....

....

....

....

Now choose one thing (factor) from your list to test.

Plan a **fair test** to carry out in class.

....

....

....

....

....

....

Planning a fair test (e)

Finding out about shadows

You have the equipment shown below:

Pencil stuck
in Plasticine

Torch

Metre
ruler

Screen

You want to find out what affects the size of a shadow.

Make a list of the factors that might affect the size of a shadow.

....

....

....

....

Now choose one factor from your list to test.
Plan a **fair test** to carry out in class.

....

....

....

....

....

....

Draw a diagram of your experiment on the back of this sheet.

Planning a fair test (f)

Finding out about the brightness of a bulb

You want to find out which factors affect the brightness of a bulb.

Make a list of factors that might affect how brightly a bulb shines.

....

....

....

Now choose one factor from your list to test.
Plan a **fair test** you could carry out in class.
Include a circuit diagram in your answer.

....

....

....

....

....

....

....

Make a list of the equipment you will need to do your test.

....

....

Planning an enquiry (a)

Finding out about conductors and insulators

You are trying to find out which materials let electricity pass through them and which do not.

You have the equipment shown below and different materials to test:

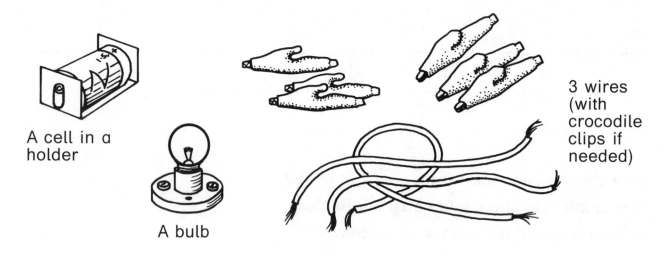

A cell in a
holder

A bulb

3 wires
(with
crocodile
clips if
needed)

Finish off the diagram below to show the circuit you would use.

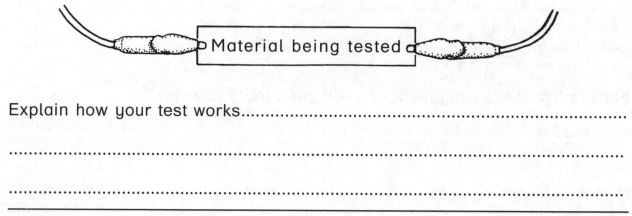

Material being tested

Explain how your test works...

....

....

17

Skill Sheet

Planning an enquiry (b)

**A group were looking at how different types of exercise
affect your pulse rate.**

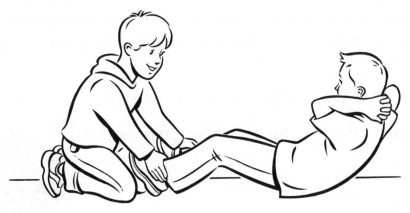

☆1☆ List four different types of exercise that they could investigate.

....

....

☆2☆ What would they have to do to make their enquiry as fair as possible?
Which factors would they need to keep the same?

....

....

....

....

☆3☆ How could they make sure that any conclusions they draw after their
enquiry are as certain as possible?

....

....

....

Name .... Date ....

Planning an enquiry (c)

Finding out about the Moon

Here is a list of questions a class asked about the Moon.

1   Who was the first person to step on to the Moon and how did they get there?

2   How does the shape of the Moon change from night to night?

3   What would affect the size of the craters on the Moon?

4   Do other planets have moons?

5   How does the Moon affect the tides on Earth?

How would you go about finding the answer to each one of their questions? **(Don't try to answer the question yourself – yet!)**
You might be able to think of more than one way for each question.

Question 1 ....

....

Question 2 ....

....

Question 3 ....

....

Question 4 ....

....

Question 5 ....

....

Choosing equipment (a)

Finding out about insulation

Have you ever had a hot drink that had gone cold by the time you got round to drinking it?

In this investigation you can find out *"Which material is best at keeping a drink hot?"*

Your job is to write down a list of all the things you will need to do the tests in class.

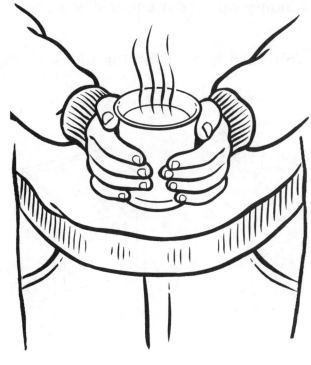

....

....

....

....

....

....

....

....

....

....

....

Name... Date ....

Choosing equipment (b)

Finding out about sugar dissolving

You have been given the types of sugar shown below:

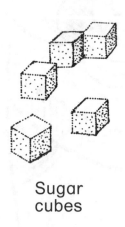

Sugar
cubes

Granulated
sugar

Your task is to find out:

"Which type of sugar dissolves most quickly?"

Make a list of all the things you will need to do this investigation.

....

....

....

....

....

....

....

....

Name .... Date ....

Measuring (comparing) (a)

Four seeds were planted at the same time.

Look at the plants that grew:

 a Which plant is growing very well? Plant number ....

   b How many leaves has this plant got? ....

 a Which plant is growing second best? Plant number ....

   b How many leaves has this plant got? ....

3 **a** Which plant is third in order? Plant number ....

   b How many leaves has this plant got? ....

 a Which plant is not growing very well? Plant number ....

   b How many leaves has this plant got? ....

Name.. Date ....

Measuring (b)

A group were looking at how heavy different materials are.

Put the readings under each of the pictures.

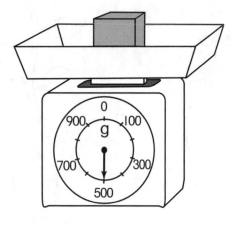

.... g

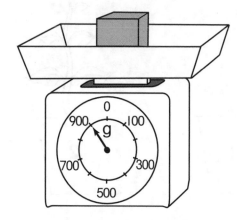

.... g

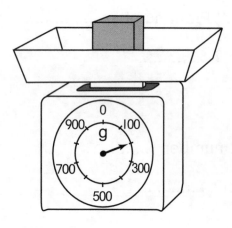

.... g

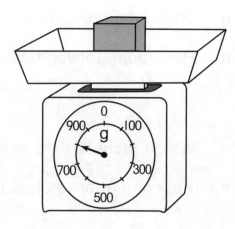

.... g

Measuring (c)

A class were looking at the growth of a plant.

Use your ruler to measure the plant.
Write down the height of the plant next to each picture.

After 2 days

.... cm

After 4 days

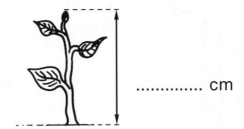

.... cm

After 6 days

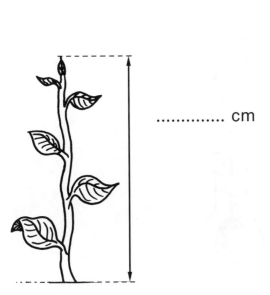

.... cm

After 8 days

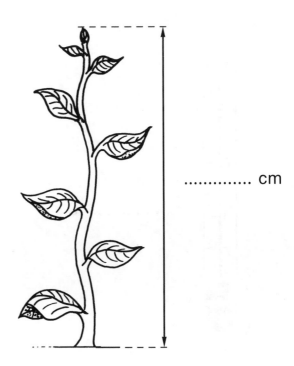

.... cm

Measuring (d)

A group were looking at the temperature on different days.

Put the readings next to each of the pictures.

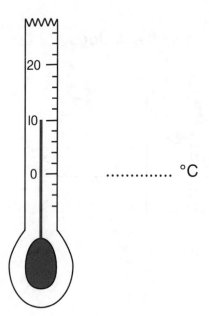 .... °C

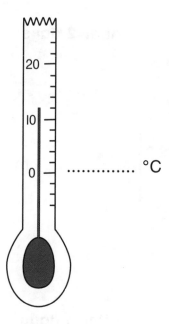 .... °C

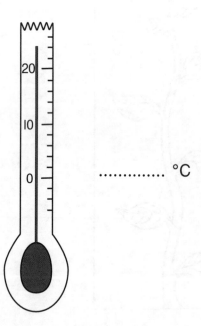 .... °C

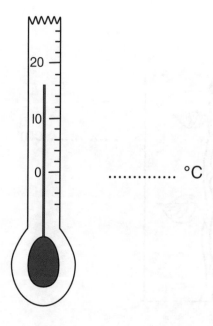 .... °C

Measuring (e)

A group weighed four objects with different forcemeters.

Put the readings next to each of the pictures.

Object 1

....

Object 2

....

Object 3

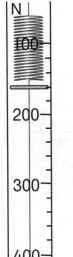

....

Object 4

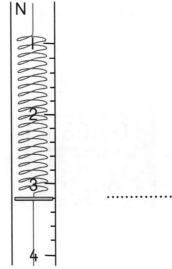

....

Measuring (f)

A group were timing how long it took for different parachutes to fall.

Put the readings below each of the pictures.

Parachute 1

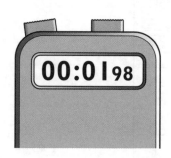

00:02 74

....

Parachute 2

00:01 98

....

Parachute 3

00:03 01

....

Parachute 4

00:02 20

....

Measuring (g)

A group were looking at an elastic band being stretched.

Use your ruler to measure the length of the band each time.
Put the readings next to each of the pictures.

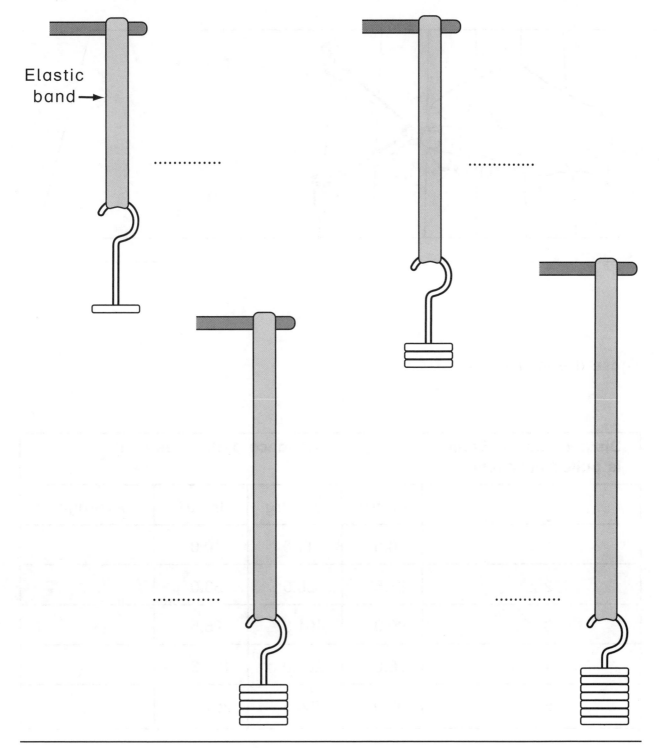

Elastic band →

Reliability (a)

Nina and Alex were investigating forces.

They used an elastic band to fire a paper pellet across the floor:

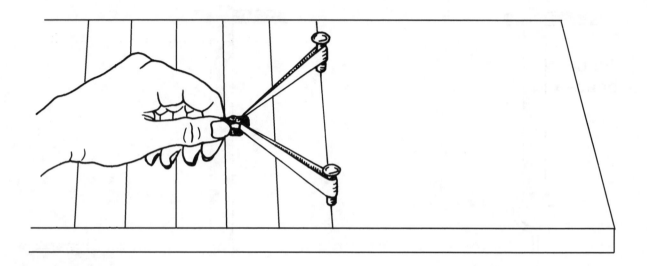

These are their results:

Distance elastic band is pulled back (cm)	Distance pellet flies (cm)			
	1st try	2nd try	3rd try	Average
1	10.5	11.0	10.0	
2	33.5	38.5	33.0	
3	90.0	101.5	96.5	
4	178.0	207.0	185.0	
5	402.0	386.5	261.5	

Reliability (a) (continued)

Answer these questions:

1 Work out the averages (means) and fill in the last column in the table.

2 Why did Nina and Alex repeat each test three times?

....

....

....

....

....

3 Which set of three measurements had the biggest difference between readings? Fill in the answer below:

The biggest difference was when the elastic band was pulled back .... cm.

Try to explain the large differences in the repeated readings.

....

....

....

....

....

....

Name.. Date ....

Talking about ... (a)

How do these things move?

Toy car

Boat

Scooter

Fan

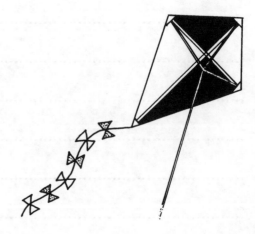

Walking doll

Kite

Sorting things into groups (a)

Assam is trying to find out which things are magnetic.

He sees if a magnet can pick up different things.
This is what happens:

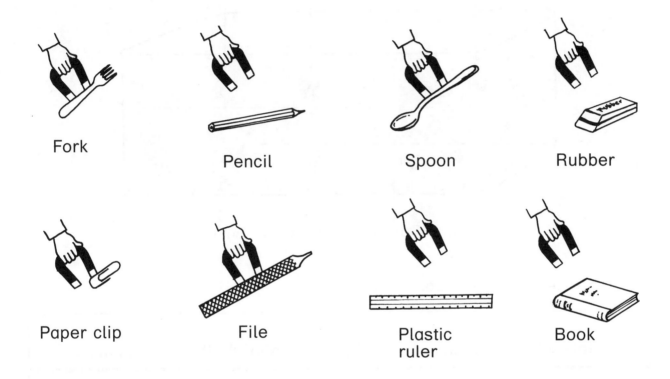

| Fork | Pencil | Spoon | Rubber |

| Paper clip | File | Plastic ruler | Book |

Fill in his results in the table below:

Things that are magnetic	Things that are *not* magnetic

Name.. Date ....

Sorting things into groups (b)

Zara is trying to find out which materials float and which materials sink.

This is what happens:

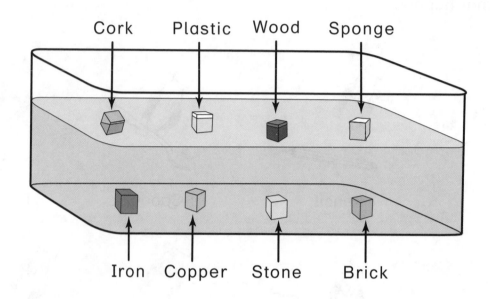

Fill in her results in the table below:

Materials that	Materials that ....

Sorting things into groups (c)

A class have collected some mini-beasts from the school field:

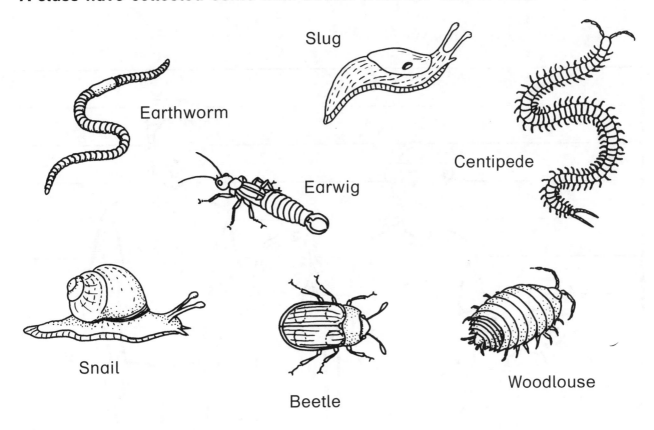

Slug

Earthworm

Centipede

Earwig

Snail

Beetle

Woodlouse

Can you help them sort out the mini-beasts into two different groups.

Put your results in the table below:

Don't forget to put headings in the top row!

Filling in charts (a)

Who is the tallest?

Put number 1 in the circle on the tallest person,
then put the others in order:

Number 2 will be the second tallest.

Number 4 will be the shortest.

Filling in charts (b)

Look at these plants:

Put the plants in order of height.

Write a number in each plant pot:

1 for the tallest plant

2 for the second tallest, and

3 for the shortest plant.

Blueprints Science Skills © Lawrie Ryan, Nelson Thornes Ltd, 2002

Name .... Date ....

Filling in charts (c)

✓ Tick the things that are sources of light.

✗ Cross the things that are not.

		✓ or ✗
	light bulb	
	mirror	
	Sun	
	TV	
	candle	
	pond	

Filling in charts (d)

Look at this picture:

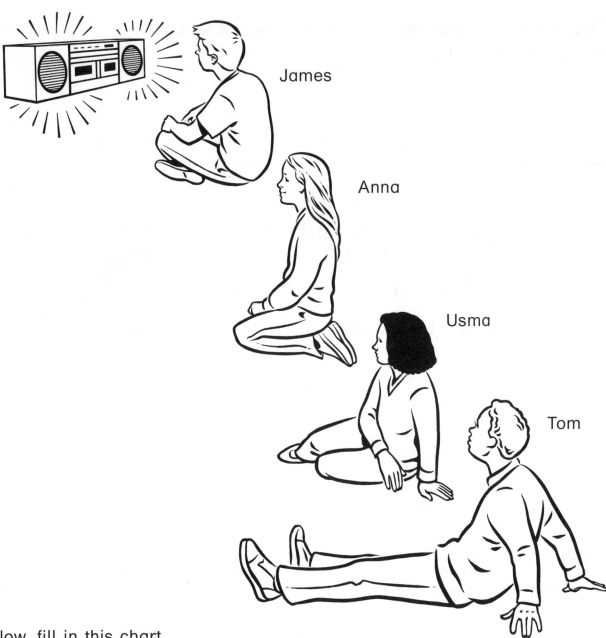

James

Anna

Usma

Tom

Now, fill in this chart.

The person who hears the loudest sound	1	
	2	
	3	
The person who hears the faintest sound	4	

Filling in tables (a)

A class were learning about birds.

They counted the different birds visiting their school field.
Here are their results:

Bird Survey

Sparrows ⳾⳾⳾⳾ ⳾⳾⳾⳾ ⳾⳾⳾⳾ ⳾⳾⳾⳾
⳾⳾⳾⳾ ⳾⳾⳾⳾

Starlings ⳾⳾⳾⳾ ⳾⳾⳾⳾ ⳾⳾⳾⳾ ⅼ

Blackbirds ⳾⳾⳾⳾ ⅼⅼⅼⅼ

Magpies ⅼⅼ

Put their results into the table below:

Bird	Number visiting the school field

Filling in tables (b)

Amy is trying to find out which things are magnetic.

She sees if a magnet can pick up different things.
This is what happens:

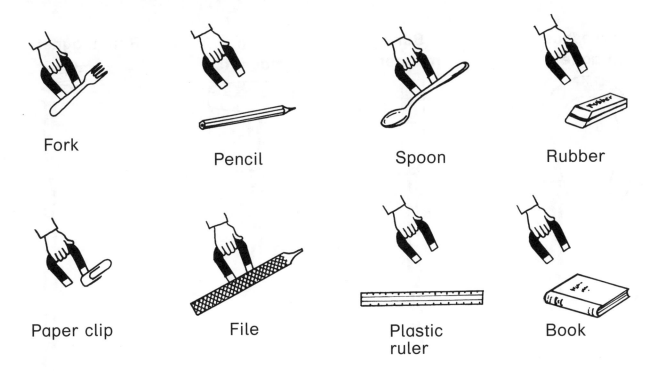

Fork

Pencil

Spoon

Rubber

Paper clip

File

Plastic ruler

Book

Fill in her results in the table below:

Object tested	Is it magnetic (✓) or not magnetic (✗)?

Filling in tables (c)

Jasmin is trying to find out which magnet is strongest.

She looks at how many paper clips each magnet can pick up.
This is what happens:

Horseshoe magnet   **Bar magnet**   **Disc magnet**   **Ring magnet**

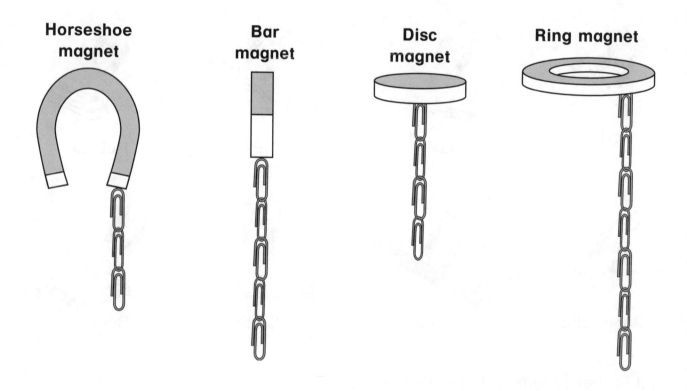

Fill in her results in the table below:

Type of magnet	Number of paper clips it can pick up

Name .... Date ....

Filling in tables (d)

Alex is trying to find out which shape travels fastest though water.

She makes different shapes from modelling clay.

Then she drops them down a long tube of water.

This is what happens:

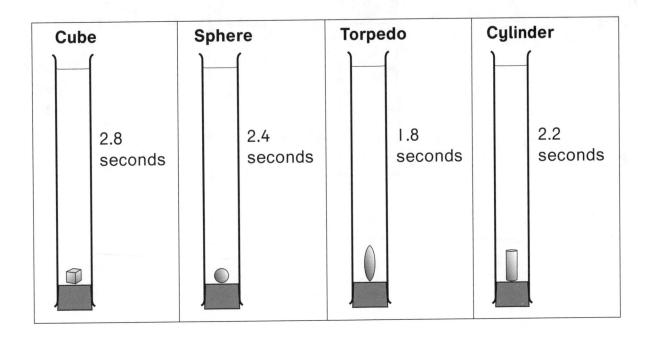

Fill in her results in the table below:

Don't forget to put headings in the top row!

Designing tables (a)

Emma and Max are finding out which paper towel soaks up most water.

They dip strips of each paper towel in some water at the same time.

Then they lift the paper out of the water all at once.

Look at their results below:

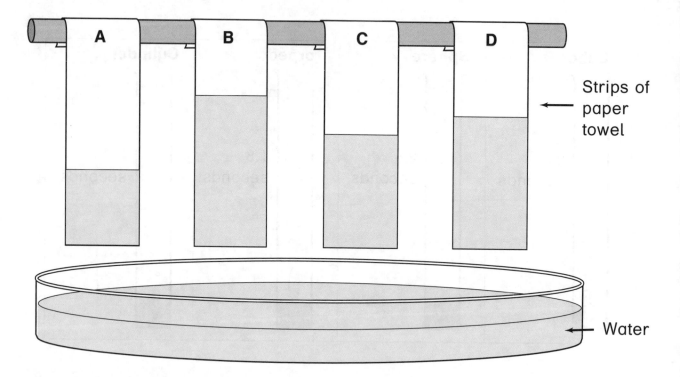

Help Emma and Max put their results in a table.

You can measure the height of the water with your ruler.

Draw the table of results in the space below:

Designing tables (b)

Sam and James are investigating spinners.

They are finding out how the height you drop it from affects the time it takes to fall to the ground.

They repeated each test three times to make their results more reliable.

Unfortunately, they didn't bother to draw a table before they started. They jotted their results down as shown below:

> Dropped from 2m → 3.2s, 2.9s, 3.5s
>
> From 1.5m → 2.5s, 2.2s, 2.2s
>
> 2.5m → 4.1s, 3.6s, 3.9s   1m drop → 1.5s, 1.8s, 1.8s

Can you help Sam and James make sense of their tests?
Design a table, fill in their results and work out the average (mean) time taken at each height.

Choosing how to record results (a)

1 Finding out which solids dissolve in water

Wood shavings

You want to find out which solids shown above dissolve in water and then record what you see.

How would you show your results? Tick a box below:

Table only	
Table and bar chart	
Table and line graph	

2 Finding out how temperature affects the speed of sugar dissolving

How would you show your results for this investigation? Tick a box below:

Table only	
Table and bar chart	
Table and line graph	

3 Finding out which type of sugar dissolves most quickly

How would you show your results for this investigation? Tick a box below:

Table only	
Table and bar chart	
Table and line graph	

For each question above, sketch a plan of any tables and graphs you would draw. You can use the back of this sheet.

Choosing how to record results (b)

1 Finding out if the length of a spinner's wings affects how quickly it falls

How would you show your results? Tick a box below:

Table only	
Table and bar chart	
Table and line graph	

2 Finding out which type of paper makes the slowest dropping spinner

How would you show your results for this investigation? Tick a box below:

Table only	
Table and bar chart	
Table and line graph	

3 Finding out how different types of seeds are dispersed

How would you show your results for this investigation? Tick a box below:

Table only	
Table and bar chart	
Table and line graph	

For each question above, sketch a plan of any tables and graphs you would draw. You can use the back of this sheet.

Drawing bar charts (a)

Jack and Vicky are trying to find out which toy car rolls the best.

They roll four cars down a slope in the school hall.

They count the number of tiles each car rolls across.

Look at their results in the table below:

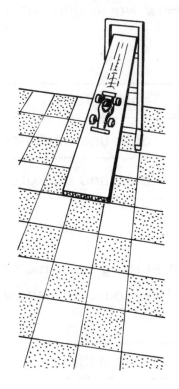

Colour of toy car	Number of tiles car rolled across
Red	8
Blue	5
Green	4
Yellow	7

Finish off the bar chart below:

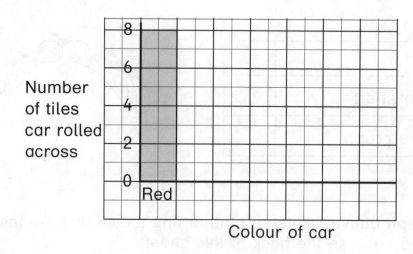

Number of tiles car rolled across

Colour of car

Drawing bar charts (b)

Jack and Vicky are trying to find out which toy car rolls the best.

They roll four cars down a slope in the school hall.

They count the number of tiles each car rolls across.

Look at their results in the table below:

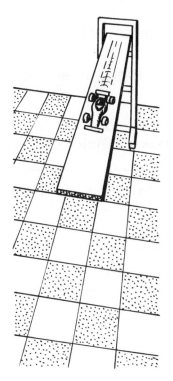

Colour of toy car	Number of tiles it rolled across
Red	8
Blue	5
Green	4
Yellow	7

Draw a bar chart to show their results:

Drawing bar charts (c)

Tom and Sima are trying to find out which floor covering gives the best grip.

They covered a ramp in different materials.

Then they lifted the ramp until a shoe just started to slip.

Look at their results in the table below:

Covering on slope	Height of ramp (cm)
Tiles	22
Carpet	33
Wood	27
Vinyl flooring	25

Draw a bar chart showing their results below:

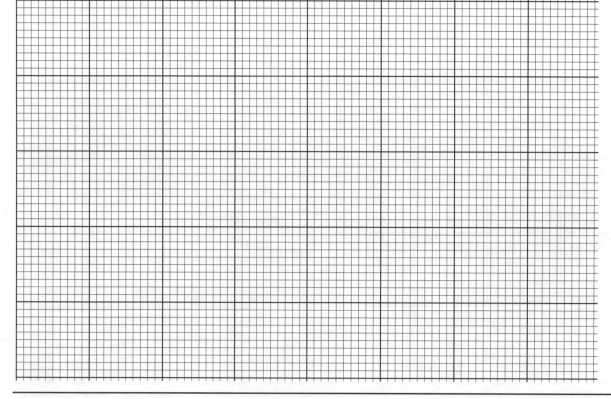

Drawing bar charts (d)

A group were looking at how different types of exercise affect your pulse rate.

Look at their results in the table below:

Type of exercise	Pulse rate (beats per minute)
Sit ups	95
Press ups	117
Star jumps	110
Jogging	89
Step ups	105

Draw a bar chart showing their results below:

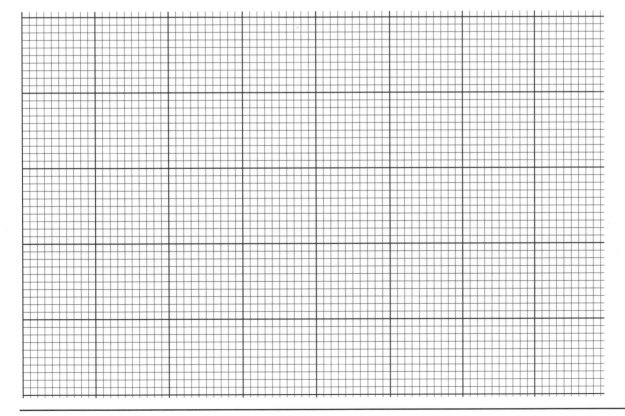

Name .... Date ....

Drawing bar charts (e)

A group were looking at which material is best for muffling sound.

They put an alarm clock under a box packed with
different materials.

Then they walked slowly away from the box until they
could no longer hear the alarm ringing.

Look at their results in the table below:

Material	Distance walked (m)
wool	2.4
cotton	3.7
polystyrene chips	2.8
straw	4.4

Draw a bar chart showing their results below:

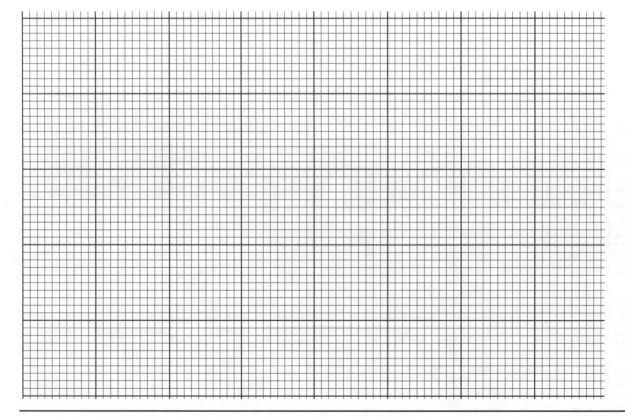

Drawing line graphs (a)

A group were looking at how the length of time you exercise affects your pulse rate.

Look at their results in the table below:

Time spent exercising (minutes)	Pulse rate (beats per minute)
0	73
1	84
2	93
3	101
4	107
5	111

Draw a line graph to show their results below:

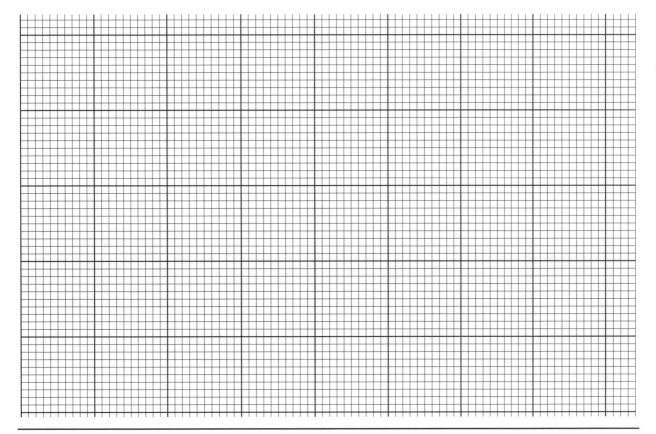

Drawing line graphs (b)

**A group were looking at how the temperature of water
affects the time it takes for sugar to dissolve.**

Look at their results in the table below:

Temperature ($^{\circ}$C)	Time to dissolve (s)
20	150
30	62
40	35
50	22
60	18

Draw a line graph to show their results below:

Drawing line graphs (c)

A group were looking at how the mass hanging from a spring affects its length.

Look at their results in the table below:

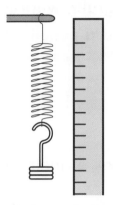

Mass (g)	Length of spring (cm)
0	6.0
10	7.5
20	9.0
30	10.5
40	12.0
50	13.5
60	15.0

Draw a line graph to show their results below:

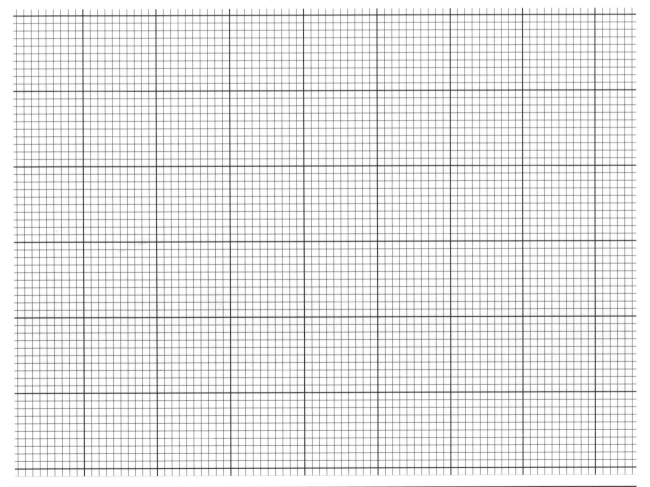

Drawing line graphs (d)

A group were looking at how the distance between a torch and a pencil affects the height of the shadow formed.

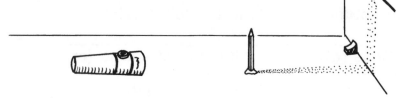

Look at their results in the table below:

Distance between torch and pencil (cm)	Height of shadow (cm)
10	75
20	44
30	36
40	30
50	28
60	26

Draw a line graph to show their results below:

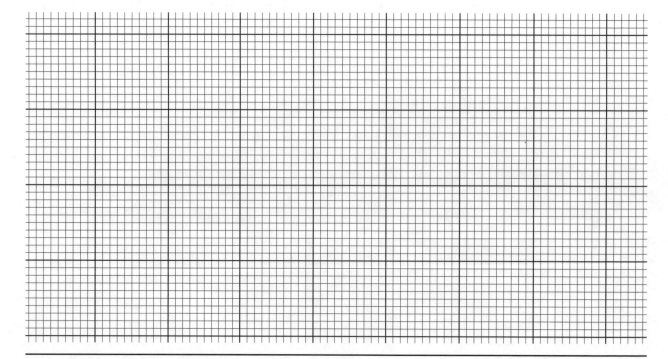

Concluding (a)

These three children had a race:

Predict the order in the race:

    1st: number ....

    2nd: number ....

    3rd: number ....

Why did you chose this order?

Because ....

....

Here are the times in the race:

Number of runner	Time to finish (seconds)
1	16
2	15
3	18

Was your prediction right? ....

How do you know?

Because ....

....

....

Concluding (b)

**A group of children were looking at toy cars
rolling down ramps.**

Look at their bar chart below:

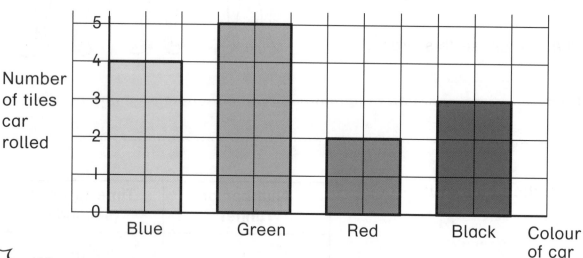

 1 What were the groups trying to find out?
Fill in the gap below:

Which car rolls the ....?

2 Put the cars in order:

1st (rolled furthest) ....

2nd ....

3rd ....

4th ....

Name.. Date ....

Concluding (c)

A group were investigating how a toy car rolls down a ramp.

Look at their bar chart below:

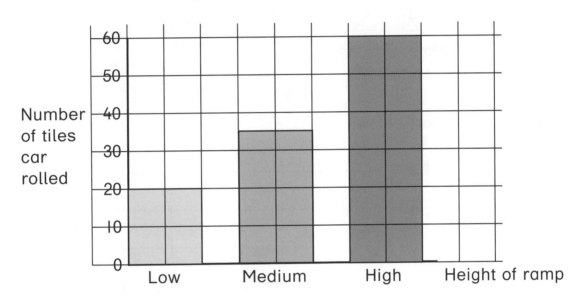

Number of tiles car rolled

60
50
40
30
20
10
0

Low   Medium   High   Height of ramp

1 What were the group trying to find out?
Fill in the gaps below:

How does the .... of the ramp affect the ....
a car rolls?

2 What pattern can you see in their results? Finish off this sentence:

The higher the ramp ....

....

3 Explain how the bar chart shows you this pattern.

....

....

Name.. Date ....

Concluding (d)

A group were seeing how well different soils drain water away.

They measured how much water drained through each soil in a set time:

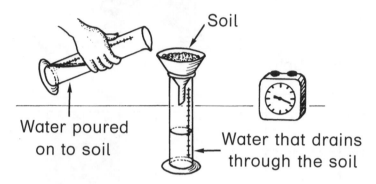

Soil

Water poured
on to soil

Water that drains
through the soil

Look at their bar chart below:

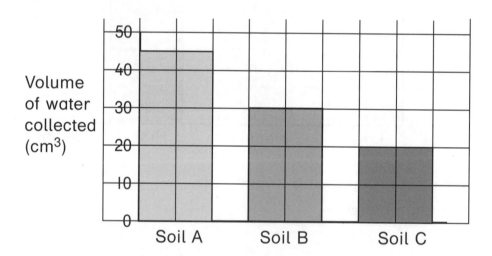

Volume
of water
collected
(cm^3)

Soil A   Soil B   Soil C

 Which soil lets water drain through most easily? ....

 Look at the pictures of each soil seen under a microscope:

Particles of
soil

Soil A   Soil B   Soil C

Use the pictures to explain the results shown in the bar chart.

....

....

Concluding (e)

A class were looking for links between measurements of different parts of the body.

They plotted their results on the graph opposite:

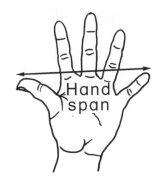

Hand span (cm)

19

18

17

16

33 34 35 36 37 38

Carl

Length from fingertips to elbow (cm)

1 What did the children measure to get the results for their graph?

....

2 What is the link between the parts of the body measured in this enquiry?

....

....

3 What can you say about the boy called Carl shown on the graph?

....

....

4 How could you be more certain of the pattern shown by the graph?

....

....

Concluding (f)

A class were finding out which material is the better insulator of heat.

They set up a fair test. They used temperature sensors to see which cup cools down more quickly:

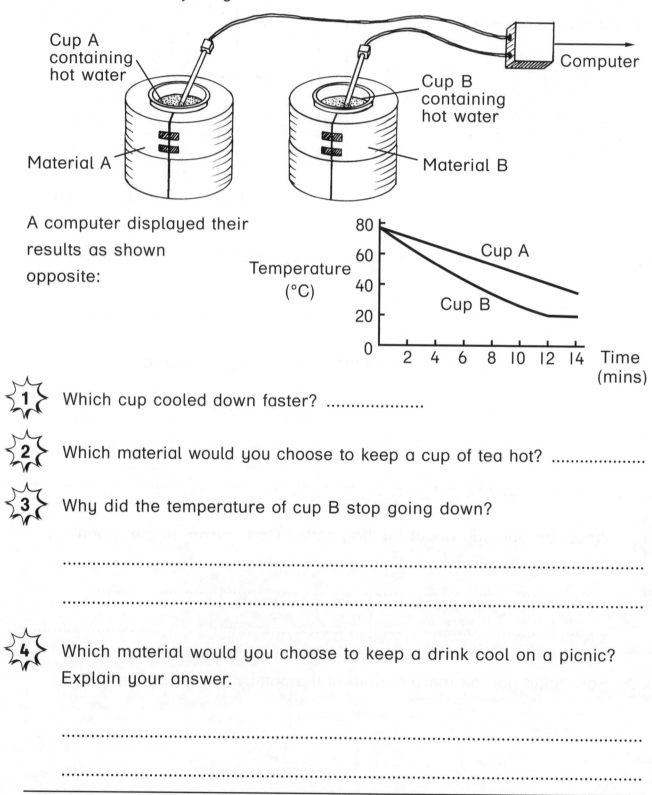

Cup A
containing
hot water

Computer

Cup B
containing
hot water

Material A

Material B

A computer displayed their results as shown opposite:

Temperature (°C)

80
60
40
20
0

Cup A

Cup B

2 4 6 8 10 12 14 Time (mins)

⭐**1** Which cup cooled down faster? ....

⭐**2** Which material would you choose to keep a cup of tea hot? ....

⭐**3** Why did the temperature of cup B stop going down?

....

....

⭐**4** Which material would you choose to keep a drink cool on a picnic?
Explain your answer.

....

....

Concluding (g)

A class were investigating how quickly water evaporates.

One group set up the test below:

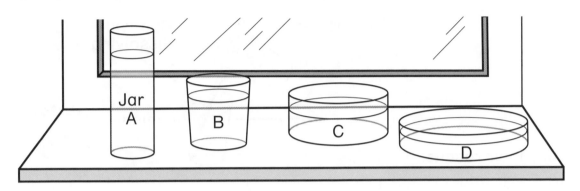

They put the same volume of water in each jar.

They also left them all in the same place, for the same length of time.

Here are their results:

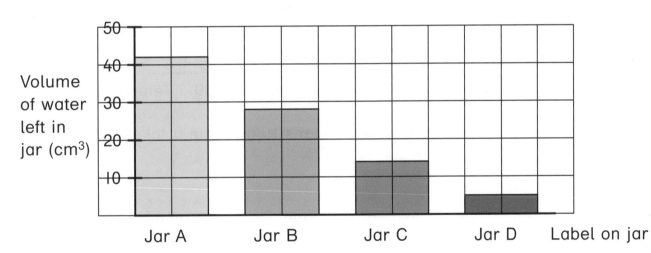

 1 Which jar had most water left in it? ....

 2 Which jar does water evaporate from most quickly? ....

3 Try to explain these results.

....

....

....

Name .... Date ....

Concluding (h)

A class were investigating how quickly sugar dissolves.

One group tested whether temperature matters.

Thermometer — Cup with sugar
dissolving in water

Here are their results:

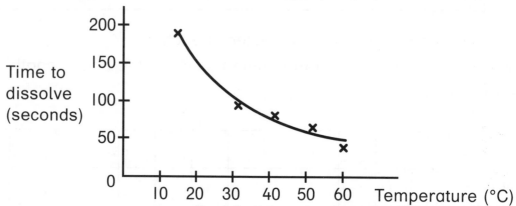

Time to
dissolve
(seconds)

200
150
100
50
0

10 20 30 40 50 60 Temperature (°C)

1 If the temperature is low, what happens to the time it takes the sugar
to dissolve?

....

2 If the temperature is high, what happens to the time it takes the sugar
to dissolve?

....

3 How does the time it takes sugar to dissolve depend on the
temperature?

....

....

Concluding (i)

A class were investigating how brightly a bulb shines.

They set up these circuits and judged the brightness of the bulb:

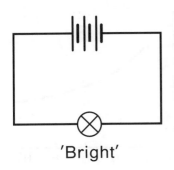

'Bright'

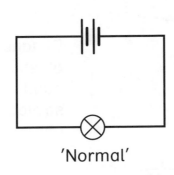

'Normal'

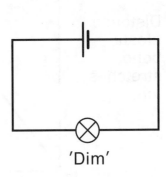

'Dim'

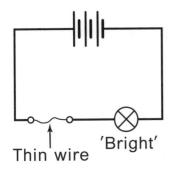

Thin wire   'Bright'

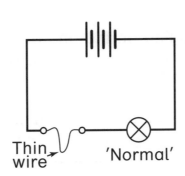

Thin wire   'Normal'

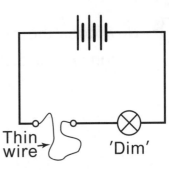

Thin wire   'Dim'

How does the brightness of the bulb depend on:

a   the number of cells?

....

....

b   the length of the wire?

....

....

Name.. Date ....

Concluding (j)

A class were investigating how far elastic bands stretch.

Look at the graphs drawn by two of the groups:

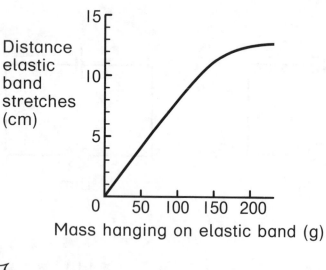

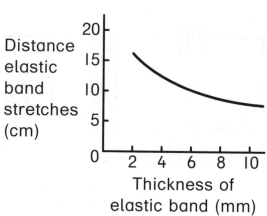

⟨1⟩ How does the mass hanging on the end of an elastic band affect the distance it stretches?

....

....

⟨2⟩ If you double the mass, do you always double the distance the elastic band stretches? Explain how you used one of the graphs to work this out.

....

....

⟨3⟩ How does the distance an elastic band stretches depend on its thickness?

....

....

Evaluating a fair test (a)

Finding out about cars on slopes

Ben and Sara are asking:

"Does the height of the slope affect how far a toy car rolls?"

Look at their tests below:

Test 1

Test 2

Make a list of the things they did wrong.

1 ....
   ....

2 ....
   ....

3 ....
   ....

Evaluating an enquiry (b)

Finding out which paper towel is best

Tom and Imran were finding out about paper towels.

They had three different types.

They wanted to see which type soaked up most water.

Did they carry out a fair test? ....

Put a cross on each thing they did wrong in the pictures above.

Name .... Date ....

Evaluating an enquiry (c)

Finding out about our bodies

Class 4 were comparing the size of their heads.

Vani asked, "Can we measure your head too, Mr. Smith?"

"Of course," replied Mr. Smith, her teacher, "But let's make a prediction! **Do you think that adults have larger heads than children?**"

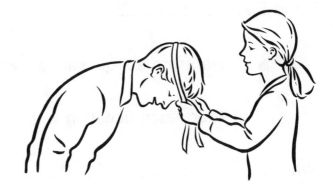

"Yes, I think that adults have bigger heads than children because your head carries on growing as the rest of your body grows," predicted Vani.

Vani measured Mr. Smith's head with a tape measure.
She compared this with her own head size.

"This shows that your head is bigger than mine!" said Vani,
"I must be right. Adults do have bigger heads than children."

Think about Vani's test.
How would you test out Mr. Smith's question (in bold above) to be more certain of your answer?

....

....

....

....

Blueprints Science Skills © Lawrie Ryan, Nelson Thornes Ltd, 2002

Name .... Date ....

Research – asking questions

We are finding out about ....

....

....

? Here are six questions I would like to answer.

Start each question with the words below:

What ....

....

Where ....

....

Why ....

....

When ....

....

Which ....

....

How ....

....

Planning my research

Before I start to collect information, I will need to answer these questions:

What do I want to find out?

What do I know already about this topic?

Where will I get the information I need?

Name .... Date ....

3
Help
Sheet

Carrying out my research

As you do your research, make notes in the space below:

Remember!

- use bullet points
- put the information into your own words
- don't bother writing complete sentences at this stage.

Research notes on ....

Investigation planner

You can use these questions to help you plan your investigation.

Think about the following questions:

1   What are you trying to find out?

2   a   What do you think (predict) will happen?
    b   Why do you think this will happen?

3   What are you going to change each time?

4   What are you going to judge or measure each time?

5   What will you keep the same each time to make it a fair test?

6   How will you carry out your tests?
    Will a diagram help?

7   Is your plan safe?
    Could anything go wrong and somebody get hurt?
    (Check with your teacher.)

8   What equipment will you need?

9   How many readings will you need to take?
    Do you need to repeat tests?

10 What is the best way to show your results?
    A table? ... and a bar chart? ... or a line graph?

Planning a fair test (a)

First of all decide on the question you are going to investigate.

We are investigating:
How does **1** ....
affect **2** ....?

Now think of how to make this a **fair test**.

Fair testing
We will need to change **1** .... in each test, **but keep all the other factors that might matter the same**.
Make a list of all the other factors to keep the same:
....
....
....
....
....
....
We will **keep all these the same** in each test.

Name... Date ....

Planning a fair test (b)

Use this sheet to **plan your method**.

This is **what we will do** in our fair test:

Draw a diagram if it helps you to explain your plan.

....

....

....

....

....

....

....

....

....

....

Now make a **list of the things you will need** to carry out your fair test.

We will need:

....

....

....

....

Planning a fair test (c)

Use this sheet to **plan how to record your results**.

 Our **table** will have these headings:

Put your units in the brackets

(Remember that **1** will not have units if you aren't measuring it)

Results

1 .... (............)	**2** .... (............)

Our **graph** will have these axes:

2 ....

(............)

1 ....   (............)

Sorting things into groups (a)

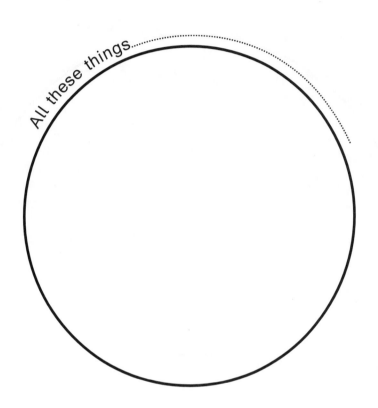

All these things...........

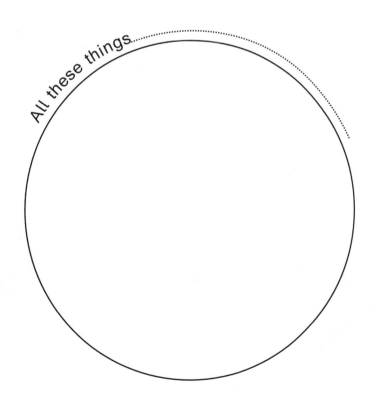

All these things...........

Sorting things into groups (b)

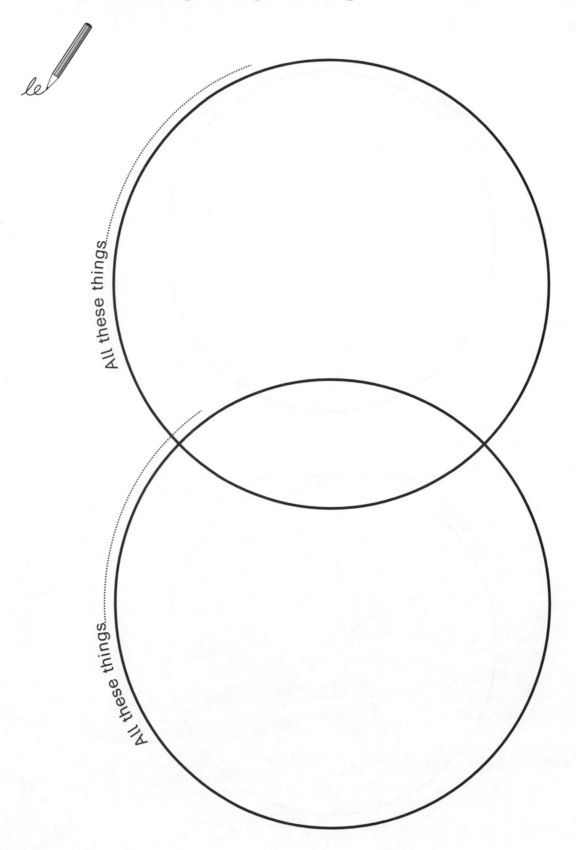

All these things..........

All these things..........

Results (a)

Put your results in this table.

You can add more rows if you need them.

1	2

Name.. Date ....

Results (b)

Put your results in this table.

You can add more rows if you need them.

1	2			
	First test	Second test	Third test	Average (mean)

After your experimenting ...

You can use these questions to help you draw conclusions and evaluate your investigation.

Conclusion

What do your results, table and any graph tell you?

a Was your prediction right?
Explain how your results show this.

b Is there a pattern in your results?
If there is a pattern, can you write a sentence to describe it?
(For example, the higher the slope, the further the car rolls.)

c Can you explain any pattern?
Try to use the science ideas you have learned in this topic.

Evaluation

How could you improve your investigation?

a Did anything go wrong in your tests?
If so, say what went wrong.

b Were some things more difficult than you thought in your plan?
How could you have changed your plans to make them better?
Explain why that would have made your investigation better.

c Can you think of any ways to improve your results?
Did you take enough readings?
Were your measurements accurate enough?
If you repeated measurements and worked out averages, were
there big differences in sets of readings? If so, explain why.

d Now you have finished your investigation. Can you think of any other
things you would like to find out about this topic?

Name .... Date ....

Concluding and evaluating

Use this sheet when you have collected and sorted out your results.

This is **what we have found out** from our results table and any graphs we drew:

....

....

....

....

....

....

....

....

....

....

This is how we could **improve** our investigation:

....

....

....

....

Science skills: record of my progress

Name ....

Class ....

Tick the skills as you can do them:

	Research / Ideas and evidence	Plan / Predict	Observe / Measure	Record / Present data	Conclude / Evaluate
Level 1			I can observe simple things.	I can talk about my work; I can fill in charts; I can make drawings of the things I see.	
Level 2	I can use simple books, with help, to find things out.	I can answer my teacher's questions about how to find things out; I can make some suggestions, with help, about how to answer questions.	I can use simple equipment; I can observe and compare things that will help to answer my question.	I can describe what I see using some science words; I can record what I see in simple tables.	I can say whether what happened was what I expected.

Science skills: record of my progress

Name ....

Class ....

Tick the skills as you can do them:

	Research / Ideas and evidence	Plan / Predict	Observe / Measure	Record / Present data	Conclude / Evaluate
Level 1			I can observe simple things.	I can talk about my work; I can fill in charts; I can make drawings of the things I see.	
Level 2	I can use simple books, with help, to find things out.	I can answer my teacher's questions about how to find things out; I can make some suggestions, with help, about how to answer questions.	I can use simple equipment; I can observe and compare things that will help to answer my question.	I can describe what I see using some science words; I can record what I see in simple tables.	I can say whether what happened was what I expected.
Level 3	I know why we have to collect data to answer questions; I can use simple books to find information.	I can use my teacher's suggestions to decide how to find the answer to a question; I can also put forward my own ideas about how to find the answer to a question.	I can measure things such as length or mass; I can carry out a fair test with some help; I can see, and explain, if a test is fair or not.	I can record my results in different ways, such as: • simple bar charts; • harder bar charts, with help; • pictograms.	I can explain what I see; I can explain simple patterns using my results; I can talk or write about what I have found out using some science words; I can suggest how to make my work better.

Science skills: record of my progress

Name ....

Class ....

Tick the skills as you can do them:

	Research / Ideas and evidence	Plan / Predict	Observe / Measure	Record / Present data	Conclude / Evaluate
Level 2	I can use simple books, with help, to find things out.	I can answer my teacher's questions about how to find things out; I can make some suggestions, with help, about how to answer questions.	I can use simple equipment; I can observe and compare things that will help to answer my question.	I can describe what I see using some science words; I can record what I see in simple tables.	I can say whether what happened was what I expected.
Level 3	I know why we have to collect data to answer questions; I can use simple books to find information.	I can use my teacher's suggestions to decide how to find the answer to a question; I can also put forward my own ideas about how to find the answer to a question.	I can measure things such as length or mass; I can carry out a help; I can see, and explain, if a test is fair or not.	I can record my results in different ways, such as: • simple bar charts; • harder bar charts, with help; • pictograms.	I can explain what I see; I can explain simple patterns using my results; I can talk or write about what I have found out using some science words; I can suggest how to make my work better.

Science skills: record of my progress

Name ....

Class ....

Tick the skills as you can do them:

	Research / Ideas and evidence	Plan / Predict	Observe / Measure	Record / Present data	Conclude / Evaluate
Level 3	I know why we have to collect data to answer questions; I can use simple books to find information.	I can use my teacher's suggestions to decide how to find the answer to a question; I can also put forward my own ideas about how to find the answer to a question.	I can measure things such as length or mass; I can carry out a fair test with some help; I can see, and explain, if a test is fair or not.	I can record my results in different ways, such as: ● simple bar charts; ● harder bar charts, with help; ● pictograms.	I can explain what I see; I can explain simple patterns using my results; I can talk or write about what I have found out using some science words; I can suggest how to make my work better.
Level 4	I know that scientific ideas are based on evidence; I can select information from sources (such as books, videos, CD ROMs) given to me.	I can decide how to tackle a problem; I know how to vary one factor while keeping others the same; I can make predictions; I can select my own equipment.	I can make a series of observations and measurements; I can carry out a fair test.	I can record my results in my own tables; I can draw bar charts to show my results; I can plot a few points to form simple graphs.	I can use graphs to describe patterns in my results; I try to explain the patterns I find, and the conclusions I make, using the work we have done in science; I can suggest improvements to my work and explain why they will make it better.

Science skills: record of my progress

Name .... Class ....

Tick the skills as you can do them:

	Research / Ideas and evidence	Plan / Predict	Observe / Measure	Record / Present data	Conclude / Evaluate
Level 4	I know that scientific ideas are based on evidence; I can select information from sources (such as books, videos, CD ROMs) given to me.	I can decide how to tackle a problem; I know how to vary one factor while keeping others the same; I can make predictions; I can select my own equipment.	I can make a series of observations and measurements; I can carry out a fair test.	I can record my results in my own tables; I can draw bar charts to show my results; I can plot a few points to form simple graphs.	I can use graphs to describe patterns in my results; I try to explain the patterns I find, and the conclusions I make, using the work we have done in science; I can suggest improvements to my work and explain why they will make it better.
Level 5	I can describe how a scientific breakthrough from the past was made; I can select information from a range of sources that I find myself.	I can decide on the best way to solve scientific problems; I can list the key factors that will affect a fair test; I can make predictions based on the work we have done in science; I can select apparatus for different tasks and plan to use it effectively.	I can make observations, comparisons or measurements accurately; I try to repeat my observations and measurements when necessary; I can explain any differences in my repeated results.	I can record my results in a logical order; I can draw line graphs to show my results.	I can draw conclusions that are in line with my results; I can use the work we have done in science to explain my conclusions; I can suggest practical ways to get better results in my experiments.